Raising Readers
WHAT PARENTS CAN DO

HERON
BOOKS
K-12 CURRICULUM

Published by

Heron Books, Inc.

20950 SW Rock Creek Road
Sheridan, OR 97378

heronbooks.com

ISBN: 978-0-89-739149-8

Printed in the USA

11 April 2019

CONTENTS

FOREWORD

In 1983, ten individuals were commissioned by the U.S. Department of Education to study the existing research and practices surrounding the teaching of reading. The overall objective was to improve reading instruction, and thereby literacy rates, in the U.S. Two years later, the findings were published in a landmark report entitled *Becoming a Nation of Readers: The Report of the Commission on Reading*, which offered a number of practical recommendations for parents, teachers, schools, textbook publishers and teacher education programs.

In 1988, a follow-up booklet entitled *Becoming a Nation of Readers, What Parents Can Do* was published, forwarding elements of the commission's report concerning the vital role of parents. These advices proved invaluable to a generation of parents concerned with helping their children become successful readers. Over the years, however, the booklet has become difficult to find, resulting in fewer and fewer parents being able to benefit from the commission's insights and recommendations.

We were thus motivated in 2018 to reach out to the U.S. Department of Education, requesting and gratefully receiving permission to update and republish the booklet. Revised for improved readability and accessibility, it is being republished under a new title.

One section, titled "Notes on Phonics Instruction," has been added. It consists of unedited excerpts from the original commission report, which can still be found online and is recommended reading for anyone interested in a full and systematic report on early reading instruction.

With optimism that this updated version of the original 1988 booklet will be of value, not only to parents but teachers and education officials, we are excited to present *Raising Readers, What Parents Can Do*.

– The Editors

Acknowledgments

We wish to thank all the individuals who contributed to the Commission on Reading and their outstanding work on *Becoming a Nation of Readers: The Report of the Commission on Reading*.

The original booklet *Becoming a Nation of Readers, What Parents Can Do* was prepared by

Marilyn R. Binkley with contributions from these individuals:

Susan Backus

Christian Gerhard

Wood Smethurst

Harriet Tyson-Bernstein

We wish to acknowledge the invaluable sections of the commission's report as relates to parents.

Lastly, thanks to all parents and teachers who continue to share with others their knowledge and insights on successful reading instruction. At Heron Books, we believe nothing is more important to our collective future than instilling a love for reading in our children.

From the Foreword of
Becoming a Nation of Readers, What Parents Can Do

Parents are their children's first and most important teachers. Children begin learning to read at an early age, when parents first use words and images to describe and interpret their world.

Because parents so powerfully influence the reading development of their children, we hope that many parents will benefit from this booklet. It is a distillation of findings from *Becoming a Nation of Readers: The Report of the Commission on Reading*. That commission performed a remarkable service by bringing together a vast body of research and analysis on how reading develops and on what conditions foster effective reading development. *Becoming a Nation of Readers* established a benchmark for educators, policymakers, and the public at large and helped create a new national commitment to reading.

Although the pages that follow are brief, they represent whole lifetimes of work. The Commission on Reading brought together the most distinguished scholars in this field, and this is a succinct statement of their conclusions relating to the role of parents. As this booklet was being drafted, members of the commission and other reading authorities helped to shape it. So parents who follow its recommendations as they set about the task of helping their children can be confident that they are being guided by the best information and advice that are available on the subject.

Parents have few responsibilities more important or more rewarding than helping their children learn. We believe that this brief booklet will be a valuable asset in that quest.

Chester E. Finn, Jr.

Assistant Secretary
Office of Educational Research and Improvement
Department of Education

Reading depends upon wide knowledge. The more knowledge children are able to acquire at home, the greater their chance for success in reading.

— Becoming a Nation of Readers:
The Report of the Commission on Reading (p. 22)

THE PRESCHOOL YEARS (AGES 2-5)

Familiarity with language is a foundation essential for learning to read.

A child's capacity for learning and absorbing language is highest during the first five years of life. Children in what are often called "the preschool years" (roughly 2 to 5 years old) develop at an extraordinary rate.

These are years of tremendous opportunity. Every day, new experiences, however familiar to adults, provide fresh and exciting opportunities to connect a curious child with words.

Talking with Your Preschooler

Conversing with children is one of the best ways to deepen their understanding of the world. Particularly in this day of cell phone and computer use and high demands on parents' time, young children are often not talked with much by adults around them.

Find time to converse with your child. Sit together at a dinner table and talk about the day's events. Take the child with you as you perform routine

HELPFUL TIPS AND THINGS TO KEEP IN MIND

USING A VARIETY OF EXPERIENCES. An occasional trip outside the daily routine can go a long way in helping children discover new language. Varied experiences help children develop different sorts of knowledge. It may be as simple as spending a day in the country if you live in the city or vice versa.

SURROUNDING EXPERIENCES WITH TALK. Some parents are constantly putting experiences into words. They might call attention to things around them: "Look at this big bridge we're crossing. Look what's below." Or they might ask, "What would we do if the bridge wasn't here?" This could produce an interesting discussion!

CHOOSING TO SAY TOO MUCH RATHER THAN TOO LITTLE. Particularly true with small children, it is generally better to say more than less. Language helps to shape the world a child knows; the richer the language, the richer the child's world.

ENCOURAGING CHILDREN TO TALK ABOUT THEIR EXPERIENCES. Talkative parents give children opportunities to talk too, encouraging them to think and converse about the world around them. They ask questions that require more than a simple yes or no response. "Why do you think those birds are sitting in the tree?" "Where do you think that dog is going?"

ASKING CHILDREN'S OPINIONS ABOUT THINGS. Be interested in what they see and how they view the world. "What do you think of snakes?" "How many people do you think there are in the world?"

tasks and talk about what you're doing. As a child helps you empty the dishwasher, hand them a utensil, saying "Here's a fork. Would you put it away?" Point things out as you travel in the car. "Look at all the birds in that tree. There are so many!" Garden together. "Look at these weeds. Let's pull some up." Explore your own home, visit a museum or animal shelter, hike through the woods.

INCLUDING THEM IN CONVERSATIONS. Adults often converse amongst themselves, excluding the children present. Whenever possible, include them by discussing things you're all interested in.

USING "WHAT IF" QUESTIONS. "What if" questions can provide opportunities for playful thinking and engage a child's imagination. Try questions like "What would you do if you could fly?" or "What do you think would happen if you swallowed a watermelon seed?"

TRYING TO ANSWER "WHY?" QUESTIONS. To help them learn how the world works, try to answer children's endless "why?" questions the best you can. "I don't know, let's look it up" can be a very useful answer. It's honest and is an opportunity to show them another use for books.

Wide experience alone is not enough.... It is talk about experience that extends the child's stock of concepts and associated vocabulary.

– Becoming a Nation of Readers:
The Report of the Commission on Reading (p. 22)

Reading to Your Preschooler

Surrounding children with books is just as important as talking. Books introduce new language, open unfamiliar worlds, introduce new friends and excite the imagination. When an adult reads aloud, a child quickly learns that a book is a wonderful thing. When an adult happily reads a story that delights them both, the experience can be magical.

Even if children do not fully understand the story or poem being read, they may enjoy simply hearing the sounds, moods and rhythms of the adult's voice, and they will incidentally and naturally learn a great deal about the nature of stories and the structure of language.

There is more to reading to children than just saying the words. It's a social event, a shared activity in which children are encouraged to ask questions and talk about a story.

Following are some comments and suggestions about reading to your preschooler.

READING THE SAME BOOK NUMEROUS TIMES

Many children will ask for the same books over and over. There are many benefits to this. Research shows that more vocabulary is learned through repeated readings. Also, the book's language patterns are more thoroughly absorbed, and new understandings emerge each time through.

FINDING TIME TO READ WITH YOUR CHILD

Most parents already know it is important to read to their children, but finding the time is difficult. Read with your child when you can but realize there may also be a relative, friend or babysitter who would enjoy reading aloud to your child. What counts is that it is done regularly and with joy.

FINDING AND SELECTING BOOKS

The available array of children's materials can be overwhelming, but it's easy to get expert advice in your local community. Librarians at your local public library know which books appeal to children at various ages. And as a bonus, local libraries often conduct weekly story hours for preschoolers.

READING ALOUD WITH OTHERS

Children learn the value of reading by seeing their parents enjoy and benefit from it. When parents check out or buy books for themselves and read at home, they set an example of reading's importance and pleasure. When they occasionally read aloud, the effects can be even greater.

READING ALOUD RESOURCES

Over the years, there have been a number of books with excellent information and book recommendations for parents reading aloud to young children. Here are a few current ones:

The Read Aloud Handbook, Jim Trelease

The Read-Aloud Family: Making Meaningful and Lasting Connections with Your Kids, Sarah Mackenzie

Give Your Child the World: Raising Globally Minded Kids One Book at a Time, by Jamie C. Martin

There are also numerous websites that provide book recommendations for preschool-age children. Interested parents might start with the two below, navigating to pages covering preschool-book recommendations.

earlychildhoodeducationzone.com

bookriot.com

There are good monthly magazines for preschoolers offering both stories and activities. Among them are these:

Zoobies (ages 0-3)

Babybug (ages 6 months to 3 years)

Wild Animal Baby (ages 2-4)

Zootles (ages 3-6)

Public libraries often subscribe to children's magazines and make current issues available for checkout. Subscriptions are also available online.

> The single most important activity for building the knowledge required for eventual success in reading is reading aloud to children.
>
> – Becoming a Nation of Readers:
> The Report of the Commission on Reading (p. 23)

Teaching Your Preschooler about Written Language

When children are read to, they not only hear stories, they learn how our language is written. If a reader occasionally points to the words while reading, for example, a child begins to learn that print goes from left to right and that there are spaces between words. Understandings that are essential to reading develop very naturally when your child sits on your lap and follows the story in the open book in front of them.

Knowledge of the relationship between sounds and letters grows as children experiment with writing. Research has shown that children

WAYS TO EXPOSE CHILDREN TO WRITTEN LANGUAGE

FOLLOW-ALONG BOOKS. Recordings of simple stories with follow-along books can be fun for children at this age. Many good ones are available.

HANDS-ON MATERIALS FOR YOUNGER CHILDREN. Magnetic letters can give them a start and offer opportunities to talk about letter sounds. Ready access to chalkboards, dry-erase boards, paper and pencils or markers makes a difference.

INFORMAL ACTIVITIES. Research has shown that children learn as much (or more) from informal activities at home as they do from the commercial workbooks parents sometimes buy.

Here are some informal activities you can do:

- While reading aloud, point out names and sounds of letters.
- Do alphabet puzzles, of which there are many available.
- Point out letters on signs, labels and so forth.
- Use magnetic letters and boards to write words.
- Provide songs about the alphabet, such as "Sesame Street: Sing the Alphabet" or "Animal Alphabet Songs."
- Build letters from playdough or modeling clay.
- Play games like Alphabet Bingo, Alphabet Go Fish and Alphabet Island (all of these are for ages 4 and older).

entering school with knowledge of letter names and letter sounds learn to read more easily.

As a final note on introducing written language, many preschoolers love to dictate stories to a parent who writes them down. The stories can be illustrated with drawings and made into books. You may find that these become your child's favorite books to read over and over.

The most important thing during the preschool years is that parent and child both enjoy their encounters with reading and writing.

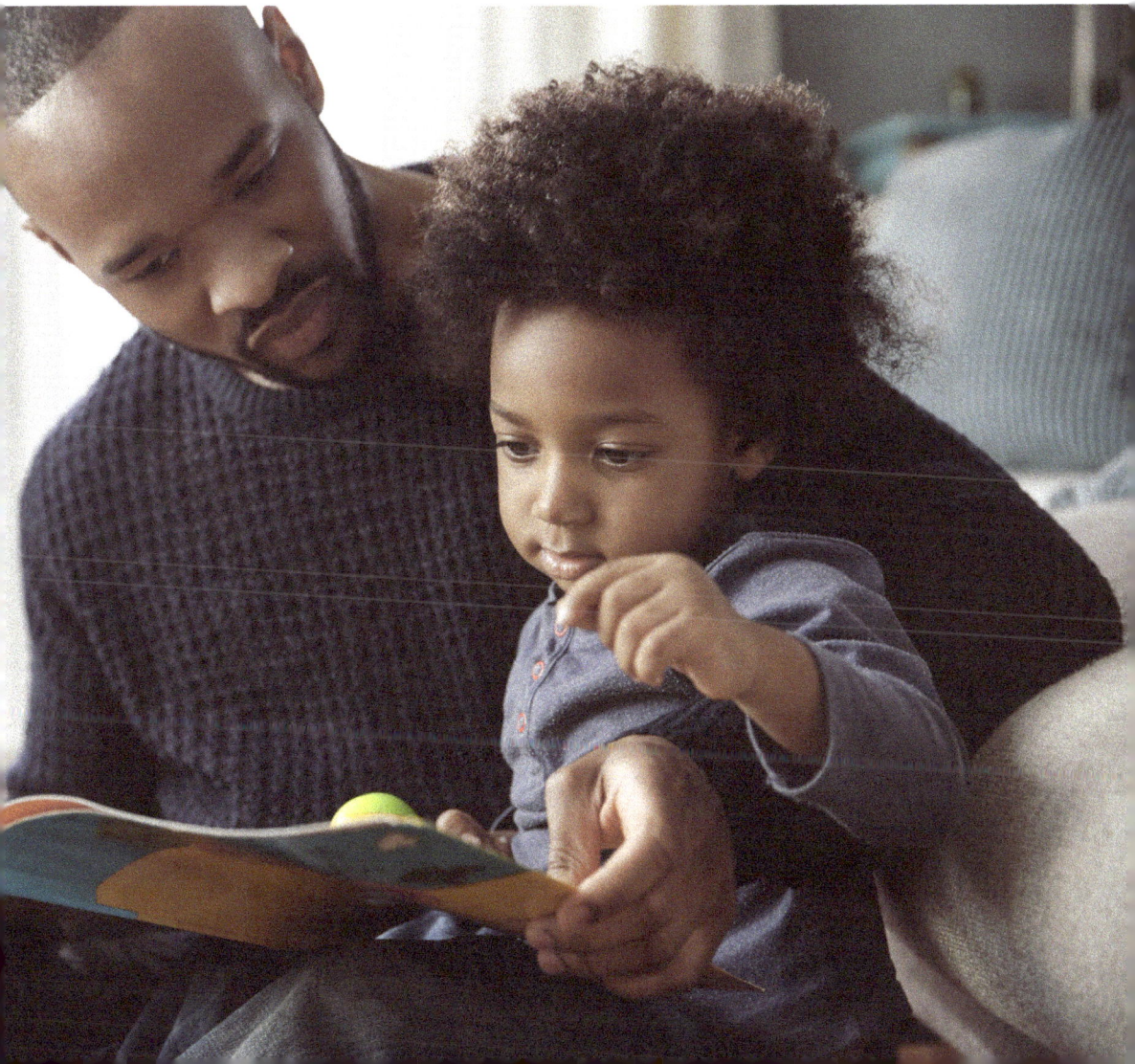

Preschoolers and Screen Time

Electronic devices are a necessary and important part of our digital world. They enable creativity and connection on a global scale. While they provide many benefits, they have disadvantages as well.

Children under five are in their prime learning years—they are learning more, and faster, than at any other time of life. During these years, a foundation is being laid for their future development and success. How this time is used is important.

The most obvious disadvantage of young children sitting in front of screens (smartphones, tablets, computers, video games, etc.) is that they are not running, playing, talking, drawing, painting or learning language through interaction with other people, and this is how basic skills develop.

Children still learn best from live, direct interactions with caring adults. Reading out loud with an engaged caregiver will almost always prove more valuable to a child than an hour of screen time, no matter how educational it may be.

Here are a few key points from recent research into the subject of exposure to screen media in children under five that parents may find helpful.[*]

- No evidence supports introducing technology at an early age.

- Early screen exposure can be formative, meaning early overexposure increases the likelihood of overuse later.

- Routines around family media use are more easily established early in childhood than later on.

- Screen time for children under two is not recommended. For children ages 2 to 5, limit it to less than an hour per day.

---

[*] These recommendations are taken directly from *Paediatrics and Child Health*, Volume 22, Issue 8 December 2017 by the Canadian Paediatric Society Digital Health Task Force. The article in its entirety is very informative and can be found online under "Screen Time and Young Children: Promoting health and development in a digital world." Also useful and informative: "Media and Young Minds," Policy Statement of The American Academy of Pediatrics, also available online.

BEGINNING READERS (AGES 5-7)

Based on 1930's research, many reading professionals used to think that children were "ready" to learn only when they reached a certain level of maturity, generally around age 6 1/2. This thinking has changed. A wealth of more recent research shows that children can benefit greatly from reading and language instruction in preschool and kindergarten.

Traditionally, kindergarten had been viewed as a transition between home and school, where children gain some basic knowledge and learn social and physical skills. Nowadays, many communities also begin reading

WHAT TO LOOK FOR IN
A GOOD BEGINNING READING PROGRAM

Every child entering a typical kindergarten classroom will have a different level of familiarity with written language. Some will have lots of experience and some will have almost none. Kindergarten programs must serve the needs of a full range of students.

Here is a brief outline of what to expect from a good beginning reading program (kindergarten and/or first grade, roughly ages 5 to 7).

- A good kindergarten program provides ample experience with both oral and printed language. Children are read to, and they are encouraged to discuss the stories they hear.

- Children are given numerous opportunities to begin writing.

- Where done, reading and writing instruction is systematic. Information is provided in an organized, planned sequence that goes from simple to more complex, with skills building upon one another.

- Children are given opportunities to learn about the different purposes of reading. For example, the purpose of reading a story is to enjoy and understand it. The purpose of traffic signs is to ensure safety. The purpose of directions and news is to inform.

- When children begin formal instruction in reading, whether in kindergarten or first grade, they are taught "phonics," the relationships between letters and sounds, and how to use them for reading and writing.

instruction in kindergarten, using simplified versions of what used to be taught in first grade. So the designation "beginning readers" refers roughly to children ages 5 to 7.

In practice, at whatever age your child enters the world of reading instruction, whether at home or in school, he or she will be a "beginning" or "early" reader. This is one who is first learning to navigate the ins and outs of turning letters into sounds, recognizing single words, reading strings of words, gathering meaning, and developing some fluency (ease). Generally speaking, kindergarten and first-grade children are beginning readers.

- The need for reading material with limited vocabulary should be balanced with opportunities to hear interesting, exciting stories that use rich language.

- Children should practice letter-sound relationships through writing as well as reading. Children in kindergarten and first grade need many opportunities to write. When they compose messages to other people, they learn a great deal about the connections between letters and sounds.

- Early writing will most likely contain "invented spellings." For example, children may initially write "t" for the word "tame." Months later this may become "tm," followed by "tam," and finally "tame." This is a fairly well-documented developmental stage children pass through as they learn to master letter-sound relationships. Because they want their readers to understand what they write, they will eventually learn standard spellings.

Research shows that, on the average, children who are taught phonics get off to a better start in learning to read than children who are not taught phonics.

– Becoming a Nation of Readers:
The Report of the Commission on Reading (p. 37)

Helping Your Child Learn to Read

In helping children learn to read, there is no hard and fast boundary between the parent's role and the teacher's. Even if unfamiliar with the technical side of reading instruction, you can happily share many activities with your children that will reinforce the instruction they receive in school.

Many of the things that parents are advised to do with their preschoolers should be continued with kindergartners and first-graders. Most important among these are reading aloud together, going places and doing things that build a child's knowledge of the world, and learning the connections between letters and sounds.

Reading Aloud Together

As your child begins the school years, reading aloud together remains just as important and useful as it was when the child was younger. Sitting close together where the child can see the words and pictures, you can encourage the joy of reading through the warmth of sharing a story.

When you read stories to children that are on their interest level but beyond their reading level, you stretch their understanding of words and ideas. Their vocabularies and minds grow.

CHOOSING BOOKS

Trips to the library or bookstore can be very enjoyable. You may want to find out from other parents and children what good books they have read lately. Once at the library, the librarian will know which books are popular with other children the same age as yours.

Steer your children to the shelves for beginning readers and let them browse through the books. It's good to let them begin to exercise some choices.

LISTENING TO YOUR CHILDREN READ

It's important to read to your children. It's equally important for your children to read to you.

Beginning readers thrive on having someone value their emerging skills. Listening will give you a chance to let them know how proud you are of their new abilities.

READING ACCURACY

If the child makes a mistake, don't worry about it, just let it go. As with any other skill, practice and experience will even out the rough spots.

If an error somehow changes the story, the child might well notice independently, stop, go back, look for and correct the error. It's good to give the child the opportunity to do this, as this kind of self-correction—noticing and correcting an error—is a useful reading skill.

Otherwise, you can just quietly supply the correct word.

In any case, rereading the sentence will help reestablish the sense of the story as you continue on.

Remember, the primary purposes of having your children read aloud to you are

- to show your appreciation of their new skills,

- provide opportunities for them to practice their reading fluency, and

- most importantly, to enjoy reading aloud together.

Family Silent Reading

Family silent reading is important too. A family reading hour (or half hour), when parents can read their favorite magazine or novel, and children can read their own books, can be a valuable addition to the family schedule.

In addition to giving everyone a time to read, a family reading hour underscores the importance you attach to reading. Because you value reading, your children will too. Don't be concerned if your beginning readers choose books that are easier than what they're reading at school. Practice with easy books improves reading fluency–an important part of skilled reading.

Consider subscribing to a children's magazine. Most children are thrilled to get their own mail.

A number of good magazines are available and can be subscribed to online. Some good ones are:

Ladybug and Click (ages 3-6)

Ranger Rick Jr. (ages 4-7)

Spider and Ask (ages 6-9)

Highlights for Children (ages 6-12)

Ranger Rick (ages 7-12)

Cricket (ages 9-14)

Writing at Home

Writing can be encouraged at home. A family message board, pen pals or letters to relatives or friends can be exciting ways to involve your children in purposeful writing.

When kept within easy reach, supplies of paper, pencils, markers, crayons, and the like are more likely to be used. Starting a journal or writing stories together can be fun. You can help by being available to answer questions about letters and spelling.

With each effort at writing, your children will be extending their knowledge of how writing works, how stories are constructed and how words are spelled.

Electronic Devices and Screens

The use of electronic devices (televisions, smartphones, computers, video games, etc.) is often a concern of parents. Reasonable limits should be placed on these.

Reasonable limits take two forms. First, the use of electronic devices, if allowed, should be limited to very few hours a week for 5- to 7-year-olds. Recent research has shown that excessive time on screens can have a negative effect on learning. Routines around family media use are more easily established early in childhood than later on.* Limits free up time for reading, writing, arts, physical and outdoor activities.

Second, if and when you do allow it, monitor what your children are seeing and doing. Focus on constructive, educational content. Watch with your children, so you can discuss what was seen and help them understand it.

---

* This recommendation is taken directly from *Paediatrics and Child Health,* Volume 22, Issue 8 December 2017 by the Canadian Paediatric Society Digital Health Task Force. The article in its entirety is very informative and can be found online under "Screen Time and Young Children: Promoting health and development in a digital world."

A parent is a child's first tutor in unraveling the fascinating puzzle of written language. A parent is a child's one enduring source of faith that somehow, sooner or later, he or she will become a good reader.

– Becoming a Nation of Readers:
The Report of the Commission on Reading (p. 28)

Monitoring Your Child's Progress

APPLAUD SUCCESSES

"Cheerleading" may be the most important role that you as a parent have in supporting and encouraging your child's reading and writing development.

You can back up a teacher's requests for promptness and diligence in homework. But while encouraging good work and positive study habits, do not forget to applaud your child's successes. Punishment does not motivate positive effort. Children will generally work harder for praise or other appropriate rewards.

WHAT TO EXPECT

As your child's advocate, you want to monitor his or her progress. Although school reading programs differ widely, you should expect clear explanations of the school's and the teacher's goals and expectations.

Any credible beginning reading program will include phonics and interesting stories for children to read. Good reading programs make a point of including good children's literature.

Look for indications that the teacher has your child specifically in mind, understands what he or she needs in reading, and has a plan for delivering those things. Then follow progress through standard channels such as teacher conferences and report cards.

WORKING WITH THE SCHOOL

If your child seems to be struggling or not making progress, ask to meet with the teacher. A face-to-face meeting at school will give you an opportunity to better understand the school's reading program and what is expected of you as a parent. When meeting, you may want to make some notes about what the teacher has asked you to do at home. You may want to follow up with a note to the teacher summarizing the plan you've agreed on together.

In the rare case where improved coordination does not appear to be yielding results, you might consider requesting a meeting with a school head or the principal to find out if there are other resources you or the school can utilize to improve your child's progress.

A school with limited resources might suggest you use an outside tutor for help. Reading tutorial resources are widely available. A good place to call for information may be the nearest college or university. Most have reading programs and provide services on a sliding-fee scale. If they do not have a program, they often keep lists of graduate students or teachers interested in tutoring.

STICKING WITH IT

As cheerleader and advocate, remember to have faith in your child's ability to learn to read. No matter how long it takes, with very rare exceptions, all children can and do learn to read.

Children thrive in supportive environments. If your child gets off to a slow start, it may not be that the school isn't trying, but the situation or program just doesn't fit your child's needs. In this case, you may need to look for a situation or program that better suits them.

Reading, like playing a musical instrument, is not something that is mastered once and for all at a certain age. Rather, it is a skill that continues to improve through practice.

Becoming a Nation of Readers:
The Report of the Commission on Reading (p. 16)

DEVELOPING READERS (AGES 8-12)

Being able to decode words and understand simple, well-written stories is a great accomplishment. But reading instruction should not end here.

"Developing readers" have learned to decode words and understand simple well-written stories. They've mastered the basic mechanics of reading, launched into more and more independent reading, and developed greater vocabulary and fluency. They're more "on their own."

This is the point at which reading becomes integral to learning. Children begin to extend their reading skills to learning subject matter from text, and good reading programs help them do this.

What to Look for in Good Reading Programs for Developing Readers

READING AND WRITING

Good programs allocate a good deal of time to reading. They emphasize writing as well. As you walk through the school building, you see reading and writing activities in every classroom and in conjunction with almost every subject studied. Often stories and literature are highlighted, but informational reading is emphasized too.

COMPREHENSION

They teach children how to understand and think through what they are reading. They teach students how to recognize when what they have read is not understood, and they teach strategies for dealing with this.

SILENT INDEPENDENT READING

Good programs give students ample opportunity to practice through *silent independent reading*. Developing readers need plenty of time for this–at least two hours a week as early as third or fourth grades. Students should have easy access to a wide variety of books and be given opportunities to read with minimum interruption. Here they can develop reading fluency, enlarge their vocabularies, learn about sentence structure and literary forms, and acquire lots of information about the world around them.

LIBRARIES

School and classroom libraries are well-stocked with appropriate, quality-reading material.

STUDENT ANALYZING AND EVALUATING

Students are given opportunities to write about what they have read. It is not enough to fill in the blanks on worksheets. Students must go beyond the text to analyze and evaluate what they have read. Writing encourages children to crystallize their thoughts in a meaningful way. The emphasis is on actively thinking about what was read or how it fits together with what the child already knows, and on communicating their thoughts to others.

Helping Your Child Succeed in School

While you always play an important role in your child's education, the *kind* of support and help you provide changes at each new stage.

PARTICIPATING IN SCHOOL ACTIVITIES

It is important to meet with your children's teachers. Some schools have orientation meetings at the start of the school year–a chance to meet teachers, establish cooperative relationships with them, and let them know you want to be informed of any concerns, should they develop.

Once school has begun, you can observe your children's classes. You might serve as a class parent and go on field trips. You can participate in parent-teacher organizations, help with fundraisers or do volunteer work. Your involvement shows care for your children and the community they are a part of.

PROVIDING A TIME AND PLACE FOR STUDY

You can support your child by providing regular study times free of distractions, and quiet places to work. Help establish a routine. Set aside a particular time, make homework and study a natural part of the day. It's not so much the hour that's important, it's the regularity.

Homework and study involve thinking, and this is easiest in a quiet place, away from traffic and interruptions. It need not be elaborate–just a table and chair in a well-lit room will do. It should be quiet and neat, with room to spread out papers and books. A stock of supplies is helpful. Pencils, pens, paper, scissors, tape, ruler and so on can be stored in a shoe box if need be. This makes it easier to "get on with it."

HELPING WITH HOMEWORK

Children frequently lack the planning skills to successfully manage long-term work. Help them think through how to break a large task into smaller, more manageable ones.

Coaching may be the most useful way to help with homework. Focus on getting the child to complete the homework, not on tutoring or remediation. Don't *do* the assignment, provide guidance.

Remember that homework is primarily the child's responsibility. Part of what should be learned is how to organize time and work efficiently on one's own, without adult supervision. If you find yourself helping too much, something is wrong. Talk it over. If need be, consult the teacher.

ENCOURAGING READING FOR FUN

It's important to encourage reading for the fun of it as a free-time activity. Most children will learn *how* to read. Whether they *will* read depends in large part upon the encouragement they receive and the example set by their parents.

A family reading hour is a great thing. So is reading aloud. The beauty of language, the poetry of well-phrased ideas, the joy of a great story are wonderful things to share.

Providing time for reading at home may mean curtailing electronics and screens. But the payoff will be gains in reading ability.

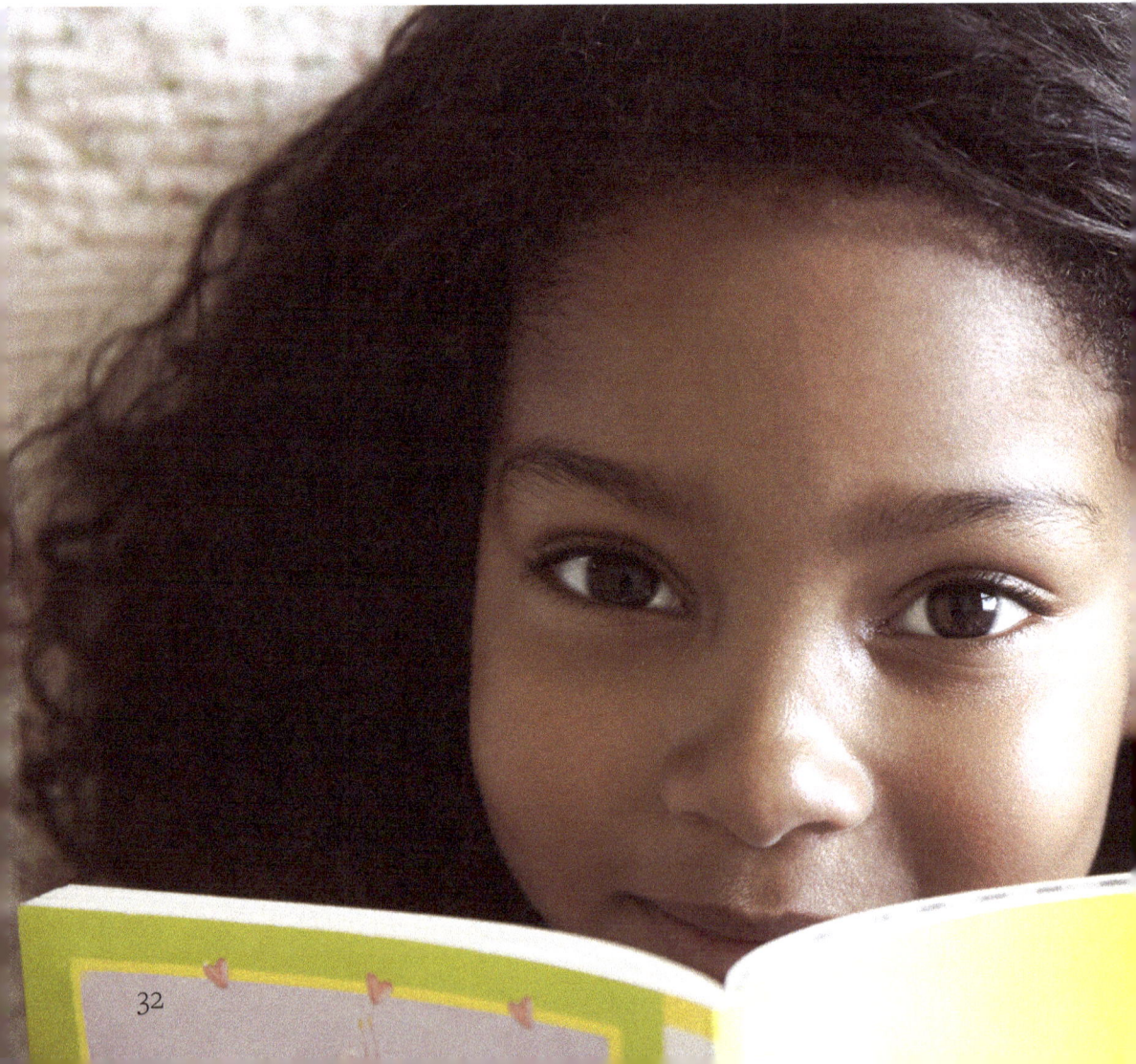

Though you may occasionally disapprove of a selection, let children choose their own books. Children read more when this is the case.

The public library is an excellent resource. Trips to the library and, when possible, to bookstores become even more important once children can read on their own. If your children do not already have their own library cards, now is the time to get them.

Most librarians are trained to help children find books that appeal to them. Some states publish yearly reading lists and sponsor competitions that encourage reading. Many libraries have summer reading programs for children. Children's book clubs have become more and more popular. And many families find that setting aside a special time each week to visit the library provides a recurring adventure they can all look forward to.

THE BIGGER PICTURE

This booklet is addressed to parents and what they can do.

The commission's full report provided the larger perspective and included recommendations for teachers, schools, textbook publishers and teacher training programs as well as parents. The original parent booklet contained a distillation of these recommendations, and they are provided here for those interested. The full report can be found online.

Becoming a Nation of Readers calls upon us all to actively participate in creating a literate society. Parents, teachers, school personnel, and policymakers all have different but very complementary roles that will help us reach that goal.

Parents have what may be the most crucial role. They are called upon to lay the foundation for learning to read through "informally teaching preschool children about reading and writing by reading aloud to them, discussing stories and events, encouraging them to learn letters and words and teaching them about the world around them. These practices help prepare children for success in reading." (*Becoming a Nation of Readers: The Report of the Commission on Reading,* page 57)

The report calls for preschool and kindergarten reading readiness programs, ones that focus on reading, writing, and oral language.

Children who are avid readers come from homes in which reading is encouraged by a parent, grandparent, older brother or sister, or even a baby sitter.

– Becoming a Nation of Readers:
The Report of the Commission on Reading (p. 78)

IT RECOMMENDS THAT TEACHERS

- maintain classrooms that are both stimulating and disciplined,

- present well-designed phonics instruction when teaching beginning reading,

- devote more time to comprehension instruction, and assign fewer workbooks and skill sheets, and

- structure lessons so that students spend more time in independent reading and writing.

IT CALLS FOR PUBLISHERS TO PUBLISH

- reading primers that are interesting, comprehensible, and give children opportunities to apply phonics, and

- textbooks that contain adequate explanations of important concepts.

THE REPORT ASKS THAT SCHOOLS

- cultivate an ethos that supports reading,

- maintain well-stocked and -managed libraries,

- introduce more comprehensive assessments of reading and writing,

- attract and hold more able teachers, and

- provide for the continuing professional development of teachers.

Finally, *Becoming a Nation of Readers* calls for lengthening and improving teacher education programs.

A NOTE ABOUT
PHONICS INSTRUCTION

The following points are taken directly from the 1985 publication *Becoming a Nation of Readers: The Report of the Commission on Reading* with the thought that they might be helpful in answering questions about how phonics instruction should be approached. All quotes are from Chapter "Emerging Literacy," section titled "Issues in the Teaching of Phonics."

"The goal of phonics is not that children be able to state the 'rules' governing letter-sound relationships. Rather, the purpose is to get across the alphabetic principle, the principle that there *are* systematic relationships between letters and sounds. Phonics ought to be conceived as a technique for getting children off to a fast start in mapping the relationships between letters and sounds." (Page 38)

"It follows that phonics instruction should aim to teach only the most important and regular of letter-to sound relationships" (rather than the exceptions) "because this is the sort of instruction that will most directly lay bare the alphabetic principle. Once the basic relationships have been taught, the best way to get children to refine and extend their knowledge of letter-sound correspondences is through repeated opportunities to read. If this position is correct, then much phonics instruction is overly subtle and probably unproductive." (Page 38)

"[A] number of reading programs...try to teach too many letter-sound relationships and phonics instruction drags out over too many years. These programs seem to be making the dubious assumption that exposure to a vast set of phonics relationships will enable a child to produce perfect pronunciations of words." (Page 38)

"All that phonics can be expected to do is help children get approximate pronunciations." (Page 41)

"The goal is for [the alphabetic principle] to become an *operating principle* so that young readers consistently use information about the relationship between letters and sounds and letters and meanings to assist in the identification of known words and to independently figure out unfamiliar words." (Page 43)

"The right maxims for phonics are: Do it early. Keep it simple. Except in cases of diagnosed individual need, phonics instruction should have been completed by the end of second grade." (Page 43)

For More Information

For further information, you may wish to contact the following organizations. Each sponsors a group or offers publications especially for parents. Some do both.

Children's Book Council, Inc.   www.cbcbooks.org
54 West 39th Street, 14th Floor
New York, NY 10018
Phone: 212.966.1990
Email: cbc.info@cbcbooks.org

Every Child a Reader   www.everychildareader.net
54 West 39th Street, 14th Floor
New York, NY 10018
Phone: 917.890.7416

National Association for the
    Education of Young Children   www.naeyc.org
1313 L Street NW
Washington, DC 20005-4101

National Education Association   www.nea.org
1201 16th Street NW
Washington, DC 20036

National Parents and Teachers
    Association   www.pta.org
National PTA Headquarters
1250 N. Pitt Street
Alexandria, Virginia 22314
Phone: (703) 518-1200
Toll Free: (800) 307-4782
Fax: (703) 836-0942
E-mail: info@pta.org

Parents Choice Foundation   www.parents-choice.org

Raising a Reader   www.raisingareader.org

Reading Is Fundamental, Inc.   www.rif.org
750 First St. NE, Suite 920
Washington, DC 20002

Reading Rockets   www.readingrockets.org

www.ingramcontent.com/pod-product-compliance
Lightning Source LLC
Chambersburg PA
CBHW041426040426
42443CB00020B/3500